Who Says Homework Can't Be Fun?

Carol George
Margaret Corboy
Susan Lippincott

Illustrated by
Jane Nichols

SCOTT, FORESMAN AND COMPANY
Glenview, Illinois   London

 ® Good Year Books

are available for preschool through grade 12 and for every basic curriculum subject plus many enrichment areas. For more Good Year Books, contact your local bookseller or educational dealer. For a complete catalog with information about other Good Year Books, please write:

Good Year Books
Department GYB
1900 East Lake Avenue
Glenview, Illinois 60025

2 3 4 5 6 VPI 94 93 92 91 90 89

ISBN 0-673-38742-9

Preface

As classroom teachers, we became tired of the regular ritual of homework. Since our district mandated a daily homework assignment that we were required to provide, we decided to implement an extension of the day's activities that would reinforce the concepts we had covered. We found that our students loved using the newspapers, magazines, telephone directories, and other forms of printed materials. On the days we implemented these materials, they perceived the work as fun. Therefore, we decided to design homework that would utilize these popular curriculum materials while reinforcing those basic skills in a homework format.

Our trial period was unreal. The parents of our students became involved with the homework and took an active part. Children who previously were reluctant to complete any homework assignment began to show interest. They were pleased when allowed to take home a newspaper or magazine from school, and their vocabularies began to soar when multisyllable words were sought. Parents began to comment favorably on how excited their children were about school as a result of their involvement in activities that were more stimulating than were previous ones.

Thus the concept of this book was born. All of the ideas that appear have been field-tested in our classrooms and have passed the test of both parent and student. Children no longer dread homework as they did before; and through the homework sheets, we have been able to keep the parents current with what we are teaching. Parents are encouraged to help their child when necessary, so that they have an opportunity to become involved in their child's learning. Since the entire assignment is only one-half a sheet of paper, the length is reasonable and appropriate for the primary-age child.

We have incorporated in this book some "No Homework Permits." Children who have displayed extra effort, progress, or achievement should be duly rewarded. Therefore, one or two class passes given out for each exercise gives that extra "pat on the back" for the child who goes above and beyond expectations. We found that when children know that extra effort will be recognized, they tend to try a little harder. We attempted to keep a record to ensure that all children who really tried were rewarded with a permit at some time.

Included are many activities that ask the child to do something. We feel that active participation is so much more valuable than passive.

Whenever possible, we have asked the student to perform a task, observe an event, listen to something special, or pretend something has happened and predict an outcome. Many of the higher-level thinking skills are discreetly included to encourage children to think through a situation and arrive at a conclusion. Today's children are not provided enough opportunities to think through a situation and justify a response. These activities will provide many opportunities to do so.

Hopefully this book of helpful hints for homework will be beneficial to you as a classroom teacher. Skills are included from the curriculum of most first, second, third, and fourth grade basal readers. However, as classroom teachers ourselves, we know that homework must fit the children we teach, and that each year the class makeup changes. We therefore encourage you to change any of the skills if they are inappropriate for your group or to make them more suitable or timely. Or, if a skill has been omitted, you have the freedom to modify and adjust as your students' needs indicate. Just a little white-out liquid appropriately applied makes you a master of individualization! For your assistance, we have included a sample letter to parents (see page v), which may prove helpful to you in explaining the parents' role in these homework procedures.

In addition, we have found it helpful to have a box with old magazines, newspapers, and dictionaries available to children who don't have access to them at home. Children are free to take materials from the box when their assignment requires them to use materials they do not have.

Please let us give you just a word of caution. These activities were designed to be reinforcing ones, not activities for initial learning. Do not assign an actitivy without first teaching the skill to your class. To do so would be most unfair to both your students and their parents. We suggest that you go over the activity first and then assign it as homework for the whole class. Each child completes it the way he or she chooses, but without the fear of failure that many homework assignments evoke. This procedure allows each child to make his or her own contribution in his or her own unique way without the fear of failure.

Hopefully this book will add interest and excitement to the normal classroom extension that we call homework, while at the same time making learning more fun and stimulating for both you and your students.

The authors would like to thank Laurie Skutecki for her helpful reviews of the manuscript.

Carol, Maggie, and Sue

Sample Letter to Parents

Dear Parents:

This year your child will be doing homework but in a somewhat different way. I have many activities available that your child will be asked to do at home to reinforce the skills learned at school. To locate information, your child will be asked to use a variety of materials found in most homes such as newspapers, magazines, cereal boxes, telephone books, etc. Each time a new skill is introduced or reviewed, a small piece of paper will be sent home stating the homework assignment for the night. The underlying purpose of this homework is to provide meaningful and fun practice while developing confidence and pride. Very few of the exercises will have just one correct answer, thus giving your child the freedom to think and justify his or her own response.

To add a word of caution, I wish to stress that the child should do the work and you the assisting. If care is not taken, you, the parent, may end up doing the majority of the work while your child observes. If you sense this happening, back off and remind your child that the homework is his or her responsibility.

The homework activities are designed to make learning fun with the family. Home learning should be a happy time which your youngster enjoys sharing with you. Parents, please remember that a little assistance from you goes a long way toward ensuring your child's future success.

Sincerely,

_____

Teacher

Contents

Introduction   xv

CHAPTER 1   SINGLE CONSONANTS
    Closet Clean-Up   1
    Your Best Foot Forward   1
    Handful of *H*'s   2
    Spotty Dotty   2
    Hungry Wally   3
    Guess What?   3
    Leaping Lizards!   4
    Big Business   4
    Suzy Shopper   5
    Bulky Backpack   5

CHAPTER 2   CONSONANT PAIRS
    Colorful Collage   6
    Designer Chips   6
    Scouting Outing   7
    Super Sleuth   7
    Name That Tune!   8
    Tongue Twisters   8

Querulous Queen Quota — 9

Flashy Flowers — 9

CHAPTER 3 VOWELS

Fill the Bag — 10

Eating Out — 10

Take a Hike! — 11

Star Search — 11

Vowel Pals — 12

Hippy Hippo — 12

Bake It and Take It — 13

Bertha's Birthday — 13

CHAPTER 4 SYLLABLES

Syllable Hang Out — 14

Huggable Homework — 14

Clapping It Out — 15

"Fill a" the Villa — 15

Play Syllable Sum — 16

Syllable Search — 16

Comic Caper — 17

Haiku for You! — 17

Get the Picture? — 18

A Delightful Day — 18

CHAPTER 5 ALPHABETICAL ORDER

School "Daze" — 19

Incredible Edibles — 19

Telephone Tactics — 20

Thanks, but No Thanks! — 20

Paper Clips — 21

Bon Voyage — 21

CHAPTER 6 PREFIXES

"Wand"ering Wizard — 22

Cycling with *Tri* and *Bi* — 22

Uncanny! — 23

Wheeling with Prefixes — 23

Submarine Sandwich — 24

Hear Ye! Hear Ye ! — 24

Jungle Jim — 25

Tons of Fun — 25

CHAPTER 7   SUFFIXES

Biggest and/or Best	26
Base Word Bout	26
Pack Your Bag	27
"____" less for Wes	27
Book It!	28
How Do You Measure Up?	28
Private—Do Not Disturb	29
Headliner	29

CHAPTER 8   CONTRACTIONS

Comical Contractions	30
How to Care for a Gorilla	30
Contraction Action	31
Tear Jerker	31
On Your Mark! Get Set! Go!	32
Weight Watcher	32

CHAPTER 9   COMPOUNDS

Candid Compounds	33
Compound Network	33
Having a Ball!	34
Compound Contest	34
Creative Compounding	35
Household Words	35

CHAPTER 10   SYNONYMS, ANTONYMS, AND HOMONYMS

Synonym Soup	36
Synonym Swap	36
Flying High . . . or Low?	37
Telephone Homophone	37
A Change in the Weather	38
Two Times Too Much to Do	38

CHAPTER 11   SEQUENCE/ORDER

Kitchen Clean-Up	39
Comic Cutup	39
Spicy Sniffs	40
Favorite Faces	40
Your Berry Best	41
Before and After	41

CHAPTER 12 CATEGORIZATION/CLASSIFICATION

Colorful Homework	42
Category Craze	42
Read All About It!	43
Dish or Dirt?	43
Urban Renewal	44
Fashion Flair	44
Place Your Order	45
Where Would You Find . . .?	45
Sorting It Out!	46
Charge It!	46

CHAPTER 13 INFERENCE

How Now?	47
Beat the Clock!	47
Smiling Faces	48
"Pick"ture Perfect	48
Toy Time	49
If . . . Then . . .	49
Let's Face It!	50
Consumer Beware!	50
A Fruity Pair	51
A Bird's Eye View	51
"Mask"erade	52
A Poor Excuse Is Better Than None	52

CHAPTER 14 ABBREVIATIONS

Abbreviated Animal	53
What's in a Name?	53
Geographical Genius	54
Cut It Out!	54
Dream House	55
In Brief	55
Street Wise	56
News Briefs	56

CHAPTER 15 PARTS OF SPEECH

Picturesque	57
Newsworthy Nouns	57
Traction Action	58
What's in a Name?	58
Adverb Advantage	59
Unsightly Search	59
Leaf Relief	60

Proper Place   60
First Impressions   61
Clowning Around   61
Probing for Pronouns   62
Homework Hunt   62
Rainbow Words   63
Noun Knowledge   63

CHAPTER 16   CAPITALIZATION AND/OR PUNCTUATION

Vera Vegetable   64
Super Shopper   64
Jet Setting   65
What's in a Book?   65
Sentence Search   66
Scavenger Hunt   66
Tally Ho!   67
Asking the Right Questions   67
Questionable Homework   68
Help Wanted   68

CHAPTER 17   PARAGRAPHS/COMPREHENSION

You Tell the Story!   69
What's It All About?   69
Wheel of Sports   70
Finding the Nitty Gritty   70
Cereal Tidbits   71
It's Classified!   71
Shapes of Things to Come   72
Scientifically Sound   72
Paragraph Particulars   73
Jake the Flake   73

CHAPTER 18   MISCELLANEOUS CREATIONS

Puppy Love   74
Every Litter Bit Helps!   74
Quotable Quotes   75
Happy Birthday!   75
Character Collage   76
Letter Perfect   76
Happy Holiday   77
Up Close and Personal   77
T-Time Design   78
Tombstone Territory   78

CHAPTER 19   CRITICAL THINKING

Cartoon Capers	79
"Inch"ing to Be Taller	79
An Unbelievable Story	80
Super Powers	80
A Perfect Pair	81
Your Opinion, Please	81
A Year Without Sunshine	82
Friend or Foe	82
Trash to Treasures	83
Sink or Swim	83

CHAPTER 20   REFERENCE SOURCES

Table Topics	84
Mapping It Out	84
Look It Up!	85
Favorite Food Facts	85
Calling Codes	86
Dream Machine	86
Strawberry Search	87
Calendar Check	87
Let Your Fingers Do the Walking	88
Take a Trip	88
Did You Know?	89
What's Inside?	89

CHAPTER 21   HOLIDAYS AND SPECIAL DAYS

What's My Line?	90
Land Ahoy!	90
Hair-Raising Words	91
Boo-ish on Words	91
Safety First	92
A Bracing Brew	92
What's for Dinner?	93
Thankful Thoughts	93
Suited for Santa	94
Ho! Ho! Ho!	94
Trimming the Tree	95
You Light Up My Life	95
Happy New Year . . . for Whom?	96
The 100th Day	96
Content of Character	97
Presidential Promise	97
You're Number One!	98

Presidential Homework   98
Downright Hoggish   99
Picturesque for Pete   99
Love at First Bite!   100
Straight to the Heart   100
Hearty Homework   101
Irish Cook-Off   101
Seeing Green   102
Symbolic   102
Spring Fling   103
April Fool   103
''Egg''ceptional Eggs   104
Scrambled Eggs   104

CHAPTER 22   NO HOMEWORK PERMITS

Hats Off to You!   105
Happy Birthday to You!   105
Keep on Shining!   106
Time Out!   106
A Whale of a Job   107
This Little Bird   107
High Flier   108
Standing Tall   108
Take a Break   109
Moving On   109

Introduction

Today homework is an essential part of the school day and has become a normal extension of classroom activities. Parents expect that their children will be assigned homework and often view it as a major means of communication between the school and the home. Children who are assigned and who complete quality homework that is meaningful and reinforcing are on their way to acquiring better study skills and higher academic achievement.

Homework, which plays a vital role in the life of a child, should meet certain criteria to be effective. Good homework assignments should

1. encourage children to explore their environment and expand beyond the material in their textbook;

2. help develop good study habits by being assigned regularly;

3. provide opportunities for divergent and creative thinking;

4. be used for reinforcement, not busywork or punishment;

5. utilize an open-ended format so that multiple answers are acceptable;

6. be creative, interesting, and challenging, while inspiring imaginative thinking in the student;

7. reinforce meaningful skills that are necessary to function effectively in our real-world curriculum;

8. encourage positive parental involvement.

Our goal is to combine theory and reality with these stated ingredients to produce homework activities that are reinforcing, stimulating, challenging . . . and fun! The assignments, which are carefully planned to be relevant to the real world of the student, have been developed so that parents and children can work together in completing them.

Throughout the book, children are asked to utilize a variety of materials—materials which are present in most homes. Since these items will be available to them throughout their lives, children should be encouraged to begin using them at an early age. Parents are encouraged to participate in the activities; in doing so, they are able to contribute to their child's learning while simultaneously promoting attitudes that will foster academic success.

NAME _____   DATE _____

Closet Clean-Up

Make a list of things in your closet that have
the letter *b* in their name.

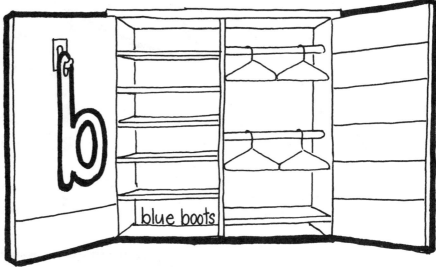

On another sheet of paper draw a picture of
the thing you like best.

SKILL: Consonants

NAME _____   DATE _____

Your Best Foot Forward

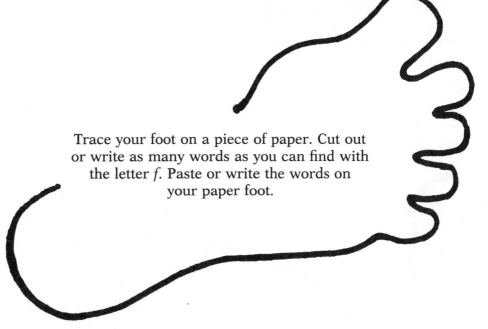

Trace your foot on a piece of paper. Cut out
or write as many words as you can find with
the letter *f*. Paste or write the words on
your paper foot.

SKILL: Consonants

NAME _____ DATE _____

Handful of *H*'s

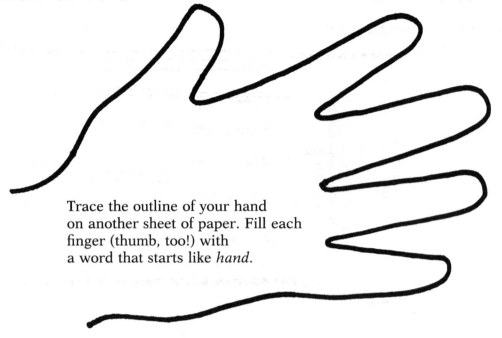

Trace the outline of your hand
on another sheet of paper. Fill each
finger (thumb, too!) with
a word that starts like *hand*.

SKILL: *Consonants*

NAME _____ DATE _____

Spotty Dotty

Dotty is a polka-dotted Dalmation dog who loves the letter *d*. In fact,
all of Dotty's dots need to have words containing *d* on them. Will you
find some words with *d* and write them in the dots? If you can read
all the words, you can color Dotty and all her dots.

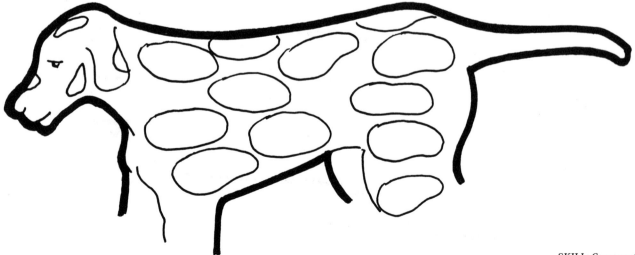

SKILL: *Consonants*

NAME _____ DATE _____

Hungry Wally

Wally Walrus can digest only words containing the letter *w*. What foods would you be able to feed him? Put those foods on the lines in his tummy.

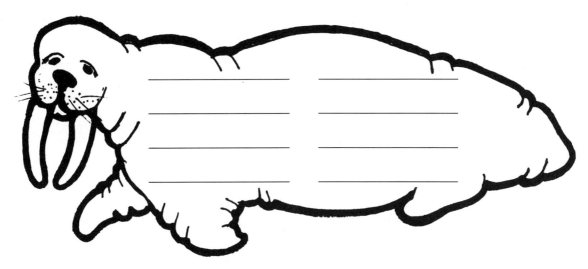

SKILL: *Consonants*

NAME _____ DATE _____

Guess What?

Find one thing in your home that has the letter _____ in it. Bring it to school tomorrow, and we'll try to guess what it is. Remember, though, you have to have some clues ready to give us!

SKILL: *Consonants*

NAME _____ DATE _____

Leaping Lizards!

Leap through a newspaper to find some words either starting with or containing the letter _____. Write your words inside the lizard's leap. Make sure you are able to read all of them!

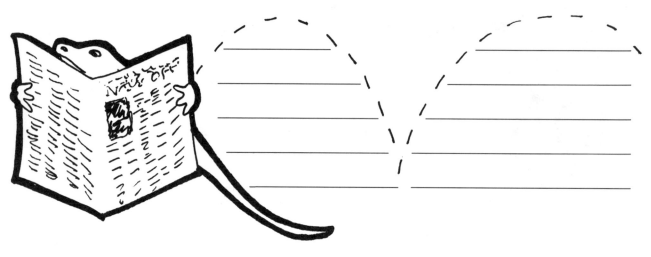

SKILL: *Consonants*

NAME _____ DATE _____

Big Business

Look in the phone book for businesses that contain the letter _____. Inside the moving van, write as many words as you can read. Can you read them all?

SKILL: *Consonants*

NAME _____ DATE _____

Suzy Shopper

Suzy is a super shopper. She is shopping for foods that contain the
letter _____. List some items Suzy could put in her shopping cart.
Write the words inside or beside the cart.

SKILL: Consonants

NAME _____ DATE _____

Bulky Backpack

You may fill up your backpack with things
you use at school. BUT, these things must all
contain the letter _____. Will your backpack
be bulky?

BONUS: Now predict how much you think
this backpack will weigh when it is full:
_____ pounds.

SKILL: Consonants

NAME _____ DATE _____

Colorful Collage

On another piece of paper, cut and paste words or pictures containing the _____ blend. How many did you find?

SKILL: *Blends*

NAME _____ DATE _____

Designer Chips

Look in your pantry or food cupboard and get some flavor ideas. Now invent some new kinds of chips.

_____ chips

_____ chips

_____ chips

_____ chips

_____ chips

_____ chips

_____ chips

Read the list aloud to a grown-up. Put a star next to the items in the list that you would like to taste.

SKILL: *Digraphs*

NAME _____   DATE _____

Scouting Outing

You are going with the scouts on a weekend outing. List as many
things as you can having the letters *kn* that could fit in a knapsack.
Use your dictionary if you like.

_____   _____

_____   _____

_____   _____

_____   _____

_____   _____

_____   _____

_____   _____

SKILL: *Consonant Combinations*

NAME _____   DATE _____

Super Sleuth

In the list below, each word has one or more
silent consonant letters. Mark out the
consonant letters you cannot hear. For every
consonant letter you find, add one feature to
Sam's face. If you find all of the silent letters,
Sam's face should be finished, and you both
will be super sleuths!

knot	write
badge	lock
wrist	wrong
knob	edge
fudge	thought
high	knowledge
though	straight
right	know

How many consonant letters did you find? _____

Hint: You can always add freckles and teeth, you know.

SKILL: *Silent Consonant Letters*

NAME _____ DATE _____

Name That Tune!

The "Twisted Pretzels" are singing some of their favorite songs. All of these songs contain the letters _____. Only you know the names of them. Can You "Name That Tune"?

_____

_____

_____

_____

_____

_____

_____

_____

_____

SKILL: *Consonant Pairs*

NAME _____ DATE _____

Tongue Twisters

You have been hired by Peter Piper who picked a peck of pickled peppers to create a new tongue twister. However, you must make every word begin with the letters _____. Can you do it?

Example: Shy Shellie should shift shells to the shiny shelf in the shell shop.

_____

_____

_____

_____

_____

SKILL: *Consonant Pairs*

NAME _____ DATE _____

Querulous Queen Quota

Querulous Queen Quota made quite a long
list of laws for her quaint kingdom. Quote
Queen Quota's laws using the letters *qu* in
each one. Write the laws you think Queen
Quota quoted.

Example: Run quickly when Queen Quota
calls you.

_____

_____

_____

_____

_____

_____

_____

_____

_____

SKILL: *Letter Pattern*

NAME _____ DATE _____

Flashy Flowers

You want to design a beautiful bouquet by creating colorful flowers.
Fill each petal with an *fl* word.

Now make your flowers flashy by coloring one-syllable words red,
two-syllable words yellow, and three or more syllable words purple.

SKILL: *Consonant Blends*

NAME _____ DATE _____

Fill the Bag

Find a paper bag. Fill it with words or
objects that have a short *a* sound, as in the
word *bag*. Bring your bag to school.

SKILL: *Short Vowels*

NAME _____ DATE _____

Eating Out

Look under the heading "restaurants" in the
yellow pages. List the names of four
restaurants that have the long *e* sound.

The Eatery
STEAK • CHICKEN
SEAFOOD
EAT IN — TAKE OUT
264 - 3735
STATE ST. ALLENTON

1. _____

2. _____

3. _____

4. _____

BONUS: On another sheet of paper, draw
some pictures of foods that have the long *e*
sound and that might be served at a
restaurant. See if Mom or Dad can guess
what you drew.

SKILL: *Long Vowels*

NAME _____ DATE _____

Take a Hike!

Take a vowel hike through your home. Find items with each of these sounds.

long *a* _____   short *a* _____

long *e* _____   short *e* _____

long *i* _____   short *i* _____

long *o* _____   short *o* _____

long *u* _____   short *u* _____

SKILL: *Vowels*

NAME _____ DATE _____

Star Search

Find *an* words in the newspaper. Write them in the twinkling stars.

How many of your words can you read by yourself? _____

How many can you read with just a little help? _____

SKILL: *Vowels*

NAME _____ DATE _____

Vowel Pals

Fill in these paper pals with vowels. Look at the vowel letter on each and see how many words you can find in print that have these vowel sounds. Write these words inside each vowel pal.

Now share these words with a pal of your own by reading them aloud.

SKILL: *Vowels*

NAME _____ DATE _____

Hippy Hippo

Hippy Hippo is on a short *i* diet. She can eat only foods with the short *i* sound. Help her stay on her diet by suggesting foods with the short *i* sound and then writing them inside Hippy Hippo.

SKILL: *Vowels*

NAME _____ DATE _____

Bake It and Take It

Dare to be different! You are bringing items to the school bake sale that are very unusual and that all contain the long *a* sound. Say what's on your tray.

Example: potato cake; snake cookies

SKILL: *Vowels*

NAME _____ DATE _____

Bertha's Birthday

Bertha is having a birthday party, and all of her friends have come. Each friend has given Bertha an *"er-ir-ur"* surprise. What do you think is in each present?

Write your guesses in each gift, making sure that each word you select has either an *er, ir,* or *ur* in it.

SKILL: *R-controlled*

NAME _____ DATE _____

Syllable Hang Out

Look at the clothing ads in the newspaper.
Jot down items of clothing that are two
syllables.

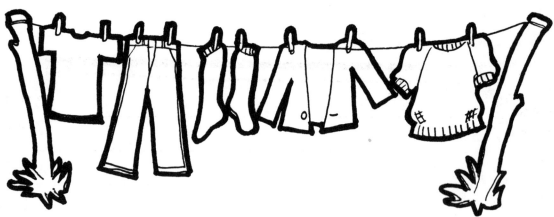

BONUS: Can you take the clothes off the line
and put them in alphabetical order on a
separate piece of paper? Extra credit for you
if you can!

SKILL: *Syllables*

NAME _____ DATE _____

Huggable Homework

Make a list of two-syllable words that have
the letters _____ and _____ in them.

_____   _____

_____   _____

_____   _____

_____   _____

Read your words to someone special. Ask the
person to give you a hug for each word you
say correctly. How many hugs did you get?

_____

SKILL: *Syllables*

NAME _____ DATE _____

Clapping It Out

Make a list of two-syllable words containing
the letters ____ and ____.

_____   _____

_____   _____

_____   _____

_____   _____

_____   _____

Clap as you say each word. How many claps
did you clap for each word? ____ How many
times did you clap in all? ____

SKILL: *Syllables*

NAME _____ DATE _____

"Fill a" the Villa

Nouns are naming words of persons, places, or things. Find some
three-syllable nouns to go with these three-syllable adjectives. Use
your dictionary if you do not know what a word means.

beautiful _____   delicious _____

upsetting _____   terrible _____

courteous _____   thundering _____

arguing _____   unsightly _____

bellowing _____   audible _____

satisfied _____   hideous _____

SKILL: *Syllables*

NAME _____ DATE _____

Play Syllable Sum

Write down names of your friends. Beside each name write the number of syllables each name has. When you are finished, add up the number of syllables in all. What's your sum?

Names	Syllables
_____	_____
_____	_____
_____	_____
_____	_____
_____	_____
_____	_____
_____	_____

SKILL: *Syllables*

NAME _____ DATE _____

Syllable Search

You need to find a map to locate the following geographical features. If you can get half of these ten features, you are a beginner. If you get two-thirds, you are an amateur. If you get three-fourths, you are a professional. If you get them all, you are a super star, and you can go and play a game!

a river with one syllable _____   a city with three syllables _____

a state with four syllables _____   a capital with two syllables _____

a one-syllable state on the coast _____

a three-syllable city north of Austin _____

a five-syllable city _____   a four-syllable country _____

a state on the west coast having more than three syllables _____

a mountain range _____

SKILL: *Syllables*

NAME _____ DATE _____

Comic Caper

Select your favorite comic strip from the newspaper. List all the
_____-syllable words that you find.

Now cut up the comic strip and have someone mix up the pieces.
Can you put them in the proper order again? Tape them to a separate
sheet of paper to hand in with your homework.

SKILL: *Syllables*

NAME _____ DATE _____

Haiku for You!

Create your own haiku poem. Remember,
this type of poem has only three lines. Line 1
has five syllables, line 2 has seven syllables,
and line 3 has five syllables.

_____

_____

_____

_____

SKILL: *Syllables*

NAME _____ DATE _____

Get the Picture?

Cut a picture out of a magazine or newspaper. Find as many two-syllable objects as you can and write them in the frame below. Then glue your picture onto another sheet of paper and hand it in with your words.

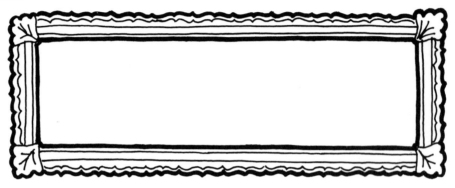

BONUS: What part of speech would these objects be? Why?

_____

_____

SKILL: *Syllables*

NAME _____ DATE _____

A Delightful Day

What is the name of your favorite day of the week?

_____

List things you can do on this favorite day that have _____ syllables.

_____

_____

_____

_____

_____

_____

SKILL: *Syllables*

NAME _____ DATE _____

School "Daze"

Make a list of the things you would have if you could make up your
own list of school supplies. Put those items in Column 1. Now put
that list in alphabetical order in Column 2. Be creative! Anything you
think you could use at school can be added to your list!

Column 1   *Column 2*

_____   _____

_____   _____

_____   _____

_____   _____

_____   _____

_____   _____

_____   _____

SKILL: *Alphabetical Order*

NAME _____ DATE _____

Incredible Edibles

Look in a magazine and cut out pictures of ten things you really love
to eat. Now on another piece of paper arrange those tasty foods in
alphabetical order. When you have them arranged just the way you
want them, glue them onto the sheet of paper.

Now write down the names of the foods here.

1. _____   *6.* _____

2. _____   *7.* _____

3. _____   *8.* _____

4. _____   *9.* _____

5. _____   *10.* _____

SKILL: *Alphabetical Order*

NAME _____   DATE _____

Telephone Tactics

Locate the name *Smith* in the telephone
directory. Find two names that begin with
Sm that come before Smith and two names
beginning with *Sm* that come after Smith.

_____

_____

    Smith

_____

_____

BONUS: Find a Smith who is a doctor.
Where does the doctor live?

_____

Find a Smith who lives on a street that has
an unusual name. What is the name of that
street?

_____

SKILL: *Alphabetical Order*

NAME _____   DATE _____

Thanks, but No Thanks!

Look in the food section of a newspaper and find five or more foods
that you absolutely hate! Cut out either the picture of or the word for
each food. After arranging the pictures and words in alphabetical
order, glue them onto this sheet. (Use another sheet of paper if you
need more room.)

SKILL: *Alphabetical Order*

NAME _____ DATE _____

Paper Clips

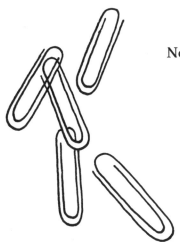

Look in your newspaper
and clip out five headlines.
Now cut apart each of the words
and lay them out in front of
you. Arrange these words
in alphabetical order
first and *then* glue
them onto another
piece of paper.

Can you do it?

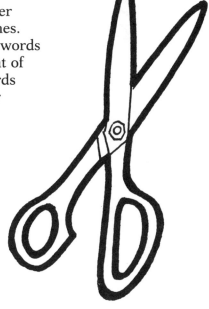

SKILL: *Alphabetical Order*

NAME _____ DATE _____

Bon Voyage

List five or more places you would like to
visit. You must visit these places in
alphabetical order. Log your travels by
making your itinerary below.

SKILL: *Alphabeltical Order*

NAME _____ DATE _____

"Wand"ering Wizard

You are an *un* usual wizard, but your wand can work magic only with *un* words. Write five or more sentences about things you would do.

Example: I would make an *un* happy person happy.

1. _____

2. _____

3. _____

4. _____

5. _____

Use another sheet of paper if you need more room!

SKILL: *Prefixes*

NAME _____ DATE _____

Cycling with *Tri* and *Bi*

Tri means "three," and *bi* means "two." Find some words with *tri* or *bi* and write them here.

_____   _____

_____   _____

_____   _____

_____   _____

_____   _____

Put a *tri* angle around the *tri* words and a rectangle around the *bi* words.

SKILL: *Prefixes*

NAME _____ DATE _____

Uncanny!

Find some words that have *un* as the first syllable and write them on the blanks below. *Now* on another sheet of paper illustrate some of these words.

_____   _____   _____   _____

_____   _____   _____   _____

_____   _____   _____   _____

_____   _____   _____   _____

_____   _____   _____   _____

_____   _____   _____   _____

_____   _____   _____   _____

Look at your pictures. Can you decide what *un* means?   SKILL: *Prefixes*

NAME _____ DATE _____

Wheeling with Prefixes

Find words that begin with the prefixes in
the circles below. Write those words on the
spokes of the wheels.

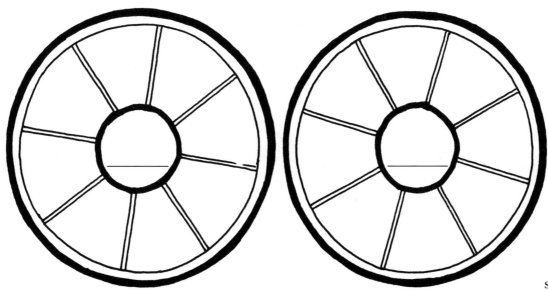

SKILL: *Prefixes*

NAME _____ DATE _____

Submarine Sandwich

Fill your submarine sandwich with words
that have the *sub* prefix.

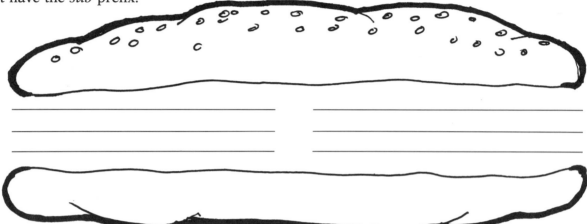

Write one sentence on the following line,
using as many of these words as you can. _____

_____

NAME _____ DATE _____

Hear Ye! Hear Ye!

Listen to the radio for ten minutes. In the
space below, write down every word you
hear that begins with a prefix.

_____

_____

_____

_____

NAME _____   DATE _____

Jungle Jim

Jungle Jim is walking through the jellybean
jungle. He is hunting for jellybeans with the
re prefix. Can you help him by writing words
with the *re* prefix on the jellybeans?

What does the prefix *re* do to a word? _____

_____

What color jellybean do you like best? _____

SKILL: *Prefixes*

NAME _____   DATE _____

Tons of Fun

You are the parent of a beautiful baby elephant! Write a birth
announcement for your bundle of joy. Use at least five words with
prefixes.

Example: Name: Repeat Disturber
              Weight: Unusually heavy

> It's a _____!
> Name:_____
> Weight:_____
> Length:_____
> Color of Eyes:_____
> Disposition:_____

SKILL: *Prefixes*

NAME _____ DATE _____

Biggest and/or Best

Look in newspaper and/or magazine advertisements and locate words that end in *est*. Cut out those words and paste them on this sheet.

Do you think the advertised products are as good as the ads claim? Why or why not?

_____

_____

SKILL: *Suffixes*

NAME _____ DATE _____

Base Word Bout

Ask Mom or Dad or an older friend to call out a word with an ending, or suffix. See if you can write the base word down in less than 10 seconds! Can you get ten words done in 100 seconds? If you do, you're a winner!

Example: beautiful − beauty   *Hint:* Don't forget what happens to some words before endings are added.

1. _____   2. _____

3. _____   4. _____

5. _____   6. _____

7. _____   8. _____

How many seconds did you need? _____

BONUS How many minutes would this be? _____

SKILL: *Suffixes*

NAME _____ DATE _____

Pack Your Bag

Grandma and Grandpa have invited you to their house for the weekend. What will you pack in your suitcase? Don't forget your toothbrush! Underline those items of which you are taking more than one.

_____ _____ _____

_____ _____ _____

_____ _____ _____

_____ _____ _____

SKILL: *Plurals/Suffixes*

NAME _____ DATE _____

"___less" for Wes

Wes must draw some *less* pictures for homework, but he does not know what to do. You know that *less* as a suffix means "without." Can you help him by drawing some pictures? You need only to give him the pictures, but you should add the answers if he needs a little more help. For example, a man without a head would be "headless." Use another sheet of paper if you need more space.

SKILL: *Suffixes*

NAME _____ DATE _____

Book It!

Find some book titles that have suffixes.
Write the titles below. Circle the suffixes.

_____

_____

_____

_____

_____

_____

_____

_____

SKILL: *Suffixes*

NAME _____ DATE _____

How Do You Measure Up?

Who is the tallest in your family? _____

Who is the shortest in your family? _____

Who is the heaviest in your family? _____

Who is the lightest in your family? _____

Compare your feet to an older person's.

Whose are larger? _____

Remember: When comparing two, you use
the _____ ending. When comparing more than
two, you use the _____ ending.

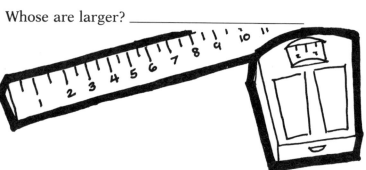

SKILL: *Endings*

NAME _____   DATE _____

Private— Do Not Disturb

In column 1, make a list of items in your bedroom. In column 2, make the items plural.

Column 1	Column 2
lamp	lamps
_____	_____
_____	_____
_____	_____
_____	_____
_____	_____

What is one thing you would like to change about your bedroom? _____

SKILL: *Plurals*

NAME _____   DATE _____

Headliner

Write down five headlines from the sports page in a newspaper. Circle all words that have suffixes. Glue the headlines on another sheet of paper. Then write the root words below.

_____

_____

_____

_____

_____

SKILL: *Suffixes*

NAME _____   DATE _____

Comical Contractions

Look in the comic section of the newspaper or comic book. On the lines below, list all the contractions you have found.

G'bye y'all!
I'm goin' t'be
ridin' the range
t'morrow!

_____   _____   _____

_____   _____   _____

_____   _____   _____

_____   _____   _____

SKILL: *Contractions*

NAME _____   DATE _____

How to Care for a Gorilla

You are going on a vacation and leaving your pet gorilla in the care of a friend. Using one or more contractions in each sentence, complete this list of warnings for your friend. Underline all the contractions that you used. Above each contraction, write the two words that make up that contraction.

1. Don't leave the cage door open because *he'll* get out.

2. _____

_____

3. _____

_____

4. _____

_____

5. _____

_____

If you want to add more, use another sheet of paper.

SKILL: *Contractions*

NAME _____ DATE _____

Contraction Action

Find nine contractions somewhere in print. Write each of them on a
line below the puzzle pieces. On a puzzle piece, write each of the
words that make the contraction.

Example:

is   not   isn't

SKILL: *Contractions*

NAME _____ DATE _____

Tear Jerker

One day when you got to school, you saw the custodian sitting on the
front steps crying. Using as many contractions as you can, write a
story telling about the upset custodian.

_____

_____

_____

_____

_____

_____

_____

How many contractions did you use in your story? _____

SKILL: *Contractions*

NAME _____ DATE _____

On Your Mark! Get Set! Go!

You have ten minutes to find as many
contractions as you can. Use any sources you
wish to locate them. Now, how many
minutes does it take you to record the two
words which make up the contraction?

_____

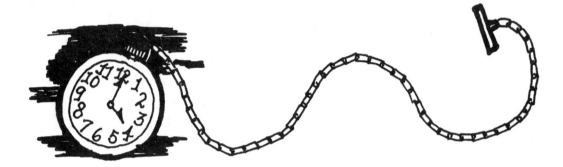

Which took longer?_____

Hint: Get someone to time you.

SKILL: *Contractions*

NAME _____ DATE _____

Weight Watcher

On one side of the scale, write two words
that can make a contraction. On the opposite
side, write the contractions these two words
make.

Did you measure up?

SKILL: *Contractions*

NAME _____   DATE _____

Candid Compounds

Cut out an interesting photograph from the newspaper and paste it on another sheet of paper. Now look in the dictionary for other compound words which begin with the word *photo*. Put those words inside the camera.

What do you think the word *photo* means in these words?

SKILL: *Compound Words*

NAME _____   DATE _____

Compound Network

You are in charge of the Compound TV Guide for tomorrow and must make up the schedule for all the programs. All of the programs you list must contain only compound words. Can you do it?

Example: 8:00 – Goldfish's Birthday
8:30 – Cowboy's Roundup
9:00 – Upstairs, Downstairs

Use another sheet of paper if you need more room.

SKILL: *Compound Words*

NAME _____ DATE _____

Having a Ball!

Many compound words can be made by
combining a word with the word *ball*. How
many can **you** make? Write each inside one
of the balls below.

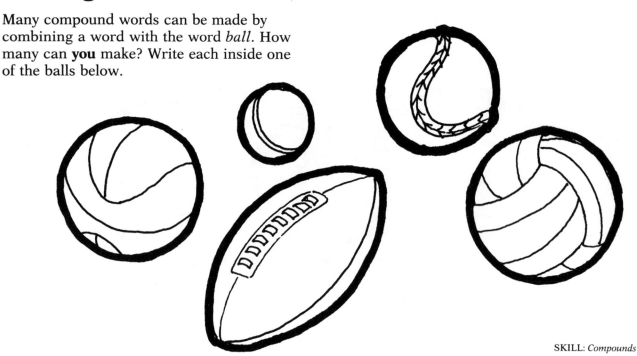

SKILL: *Compounds*

NAME _____ DATE _____

Compound Contest

Search for compound words in print. Use
whatever source you choose. List your words
below and **double-check** your spelling!

Note: The one with the most compounds gets
a **No Homework** pass!

_____

_____

_____

_____

_____

_____

SKILL: *Compounds*

NAME _____ DATE _____

Creative Compounding

Look in old magazines and cut out pictures to make some compound words. On another sheet of paper, paste the pictures side by side and label your compound words.

Example: a picture of a cup and a picture of a cake would make a cupcake.

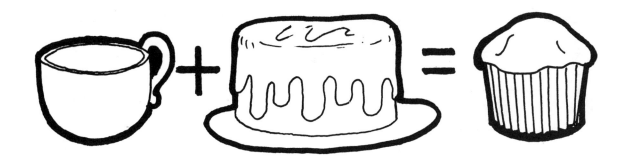

SKILL: Compounds

NAME _____ DATE _____

Household Words

Search your house for compound words. How many things can you find that are made up of two smaller words? Write those household words inside the house.

Examples: doorknob; fireplace

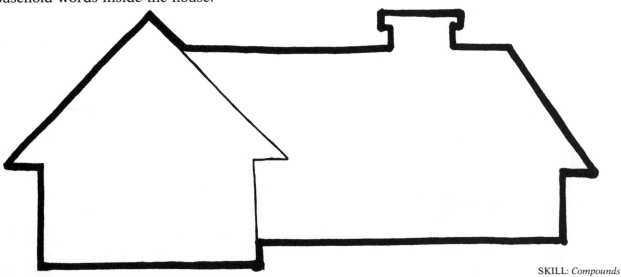

SKILL: Compounds

NAME _____   DATE _____

Synonym Soup

Look in a magazine and copy
three or more slogans from
advertisements. Underline one
word in each slogan and write a
synonym above it.

                              Stretch
                Example: <u>Reach</u> out and touch someone.

SKILL: *Synonyns*

NAME _____   DATE _____

Synonym Swap

Synonyms are words that mean the same.
Cut out one paragraph from a magazine
and circle five or more words. Glue this
paragraph onto this sheet. Now go back and
write a synonym for each of your circled
words.

Does substituting the words change the

meaning of your paragraph? _____

SKILL: *Synonyms*

NAME _____ DATE _____

Flying High . . . or Low?

Design a kite with a tail. You may use any materials you wish. Make the tail out of antonym pairs. See how long you can make the tail of your kite in _____ minutes.

SKILL: *Antonyms*

NAME _____ DATE _____

Telephone Homophone

Mother was too busy to go to the market, so she phoned home and asked you to go for her. As she talked, she gave you the shopping list to write down. Let's see what you wrote.

Example:

1. **Four** rolls **for** hamburger buns.

2. _____ hot dogs because the dogs _____ all but one of them.

3. Fresh _____ to fix for the track _____.

4. _____ to use to bake bread to put on the table by the _____ in the vase.

5. _____ berries for the baby who _____ out all the birthday candles.

6. A _____ popsicle for you because you _____ ten library books this week.

BONUS Now you can make up a list for Mom using homophones.

SKILL: *Homophones*

NAME _____   DATE _____

A Change in the Weather

Clip out a weather report and glue it to this page. Cross out any words that can be replaced with an antonym. Now write an antonym above each word you have crossed out. Does altering these words change the weather forecast?

SKILL: Antonyms

NAME _____   DATE _____

Two Times Too Much to Do

Finish this story using *to, two,* and *too*: On Tuesday afternoon, my teacher gave me an assignment that I couldn't believe. Let me tell you about it.

_____

_____

_____

_____

_____

_____

_____

SKILL: Homonyms

NAME _____ DATE _____

Kitchen Clean-Up

Help your parents
by washing the dishes.
Now list the steps
you followed.

First I _____

Next I _____

Then I _____

Next I _____

Finally I _____

BONUS Tell how to mop the floor.

SKILL: *Sequence*

NAME _____ DATE _____

Comic Cutup

Cut up your favorite comic strip and have
someone mix up the pieces. Can you put the
pieces back in the proper sequence? Tape or
paste them to a separate sheet of paper.

What is the name of your favorite comic
strip?

_____

Which comic strip do you like the least?

_____

SKILL: *Sequence*

NAME _____ DATE _____

Spicy Sniffs

Select five spices from the spice rack. Arrange them in order from the best smelling to the worst smelling. Copy their names below.

Spices

Best smelling _____

_____

_____

_____

Worst smelling _____

SKILL: *Ordering*

NAME _____ DATE _____

Favorite Faces

Who are your five favorite television characters? Rank them in order from the one you like most (1) to the one you like least (5).

1. _____

2. _____

3. _____

4. _____

5. _____

BONUS Now turn this sheet over or use another sheet of paper and write those five characters in alphabetical order.

SKILL: *Ordering*

NAME _____   DATE _____

Your Berry Best

List some delicious foods you can make with strawberries. Choose your favorite food and write your own recipe below.

_____

_____

_____

_____

_____

_____

SKILL: *Sequencing*

NAME _____   DATE _____

Before and After

Cut out a picture that shows someone doing something. Now tell what you think happened before the picture and after the picture.

SKILL: *Sequencing*

NAME _____ DATE _____

Colorful Homework

List objects that are usually these colors.

Blue   *Red*

_____   _____

_____   _____

_____   _____

Yellow   *Green*

_____   _____

_____   _____

_____   _____

_____   _____

SKILL: *Categorizing*

NAME _____ DATE _____

Category Craze

Choose the correct answer for each block. The "l" column shows you how.

	l	b	c	r	s	t
nouns	lamp					
verbs	lick					
adjectives	little					
adverbs	loudly					

You may take out the letters and add others, or you may take out the nouns on top and add parts of speech. You and your teacher can decide the category you want to use.

SKILL: *Categorizing*

NAME _____   DATE _____

Read All About It!

Tiny Tim's wife just had twins. He needs help naming these twins. One is a boy, and the other is a girl. Tiny Tim was hoping to have the names start with a *T* as his name does. Any suggestions?

Baby Boy's Names   *Baby Girl's Names*

_____   _____

_____   _____

_____   _____

_____   _____

_____   _____

_____   _____

SKILL: *Classifying*

NAME _____   DATE _____

Dish or Dirt?

In your dictionary look up the words below, and read the definitions carefully.

larch   hors d'oeuvre   escarole

begonia   geranium   ambrosia

Which will you plant, and which will you eat?

Plant   *Eat*

_____   _____

_____   _____

_____   _____

SKILL: *Categorization*

NAME _____ DATE _____

Urban Renewal

Let's remodel your bedroom. Find pictures of furniture in magazines, newspapers, or old catalogs. Cut and paste the pieces of furniture you'd like in your new bedroom. Don't forget the bed! Use another sheet of paper if you need more room.

SKILL: *Classification*

NAME _____ DATE _____

Fashion Flair

You may create a new wardrobe. Look in a catalog and cut out as many different articles of clothing as you would like to have. Arrange them in order from the cheapest to the most expensive. Paste them below or on another piece of paper. Let everyone see the new you!

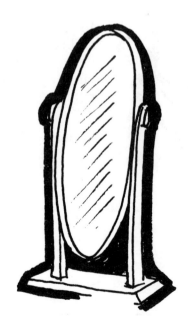

SKILL: *Categorization*

NAME _____ DATE _____

Place Your Order

Cut out ten or more objects. Now decide on
a way to classify them. You might decide to
arrange them according to height, size,
color, shape, or cost. It's your decision. After
you decide, paste each in its proper place,
and then see if someone in your home can
determine what classification you used.
Use a separate sheet of paper if you need
more room.

SKILL: *Categorizing*

NAME _____ DATE _____

Where Would You Find . . . ?

Ask an adult if you can look in a cookbook
or recipe box to answer the following
questions:

How many different categories or chapters are there? _____

Which category or chapter has the most recipes? _____

Which category has the fewest recipes? _____

Where would you look to find out how to make banana bread?

_____

What was the most unusual recipe you found? _____

What category looks the most tasty? _____

Which category looks the most unappetizing? _____

SKILL: *Categorizing*

NAME _____ DATE _____

Sorting It Out!

Locate an appealing recipe in a cookbook. Categorize the ingredients
by using the table below.

Liquid Ingredients	Dry Ingredients	Equipment
_____	_____	_____
_____	_____	_____
_____	_____	_____
_____	_____	_____
_____	_____	_____
_____	_____	_____
_____	_____	_____

SKILL: *Categorizing*

NAME _____ DATE _____

Charge It!

You have been given your own **Super Charge**
card. Select some items you might purchase
in these areas of a department store.

Housewares	Sporting Goods	Clothing	Jewelry
_____	_____	_____	_____
_____	_____	_____	_____
_____	_____	_____	_____
_____	_____	_____	_____

SKILL: *Classifying*

NAME _____   DATE _____

How Now?

Interview a grandparent or another older
person to find out what school days were like
when that person went to school. How were
those days like yours? How were they
different?

_____

_____

_____

_____

_____

_____

_____

SKILL: *Compare/Contrast*

NAME _____   DATE _____

Beat the Clock!

You are trapped inside a windowless
building that will be destroyed by bulldozers
in just thirty minutes! You **must** get a
message through a tiny crack in the wall so
the workmen will know you are inside and
will delay razing the building. You have only
a magazine, a pair of scissors, a bottle of
glue, a piece of paper, and thirty minutes.
Set your timer (or watch the clock) and get
busy! You will need a separate piece of
paper.

SKILL: *Cause/Effect*

NAME _____ DATE _____

Smiling Faces

Look in your favorite section of the newspaper. Count the number
of smiling faces in that section. How many smiling faces did you
see? _____

Cut out one of those faces and tell why that person is smiling.
(Remember to use complete sentences.) Attach your picture to this
paper.

_____

_____

SKILL: *Drawing Conclusions*

NAME _____ DATE _____

"Pick"ture Perfect

Create a design using toothpicks. Glue this design onto another sheet
of paper. If you could use this creation for any purpose, what would
that purpose be? Remember, you can have it be anything you wish,
and it can be used in any way! Use your imagination to write about
your creation on this sheet. (Don't forget the title!)

_____

_____

_____

_____

_____

_____

SKILL: *Predicting Outcomes*

NAME _____   DATE _____

Toy Time

Cut out a picture of a sleek new toy. Draw a picture of how the toy will look after the most careless kid in the neighborhood plays with it for awhile. Describe it.

SKILL: *Predicting Outcomes*

NAME _____   DATE _____

If . . . Then . . .

Cut out pictures of some products in a magazine, and tell the result of not using them.

Example: If you don't brush with Sparkle Toothpaste, then your teeth will rot. (You may use another sheet of paper if you need more room.)

SKILL: *Cause/Effect*

NAME _____ DATE _____

Let's Face It!

We can usually tell how people feel by how they look. Cut out some pictures of people who are sad, worried, excited, angry, or scared. Now paste these pictures on a larger sheet of paper and label each one with the correct feeling.

SKILL: *Interpreting Feelings*

NAME _____ DATE _____

Consumer Beware!

List five or more words that make you **not** want to buy a product that you have seen on television. These words may or may not be in the advertisements.

SKILL: *Drawing Conclusions*

NAME _____ DATE _____

A Fruity Pair

Draw a picture of two kinds of fruits. Look
at them very closely. On the lines below,
compare and contrast these two fruits.
Compare means to tell how they are alike.
Contrast means to tell how they are different.

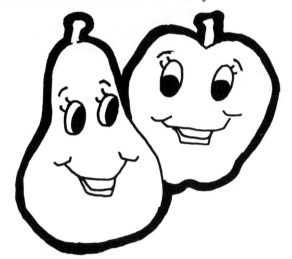

_____

_____

_____

_____

_____

_____

_____

SKILL: *Compare/Contrast*

NAME _____ DATE _____

A Bird's Eye View

Pretend you are a kite flying in the March winds. Write down some
of the things you might see when flying over a farm.

_____

_____

Now pretend you are flying over a big city. Record the things you
might see here that you would not see on a farm.

_____

_____

How would flying over a farm and flying over a city be alike?

_____

How might they be different? _____

_____

SKILL: *Compare/Contrast*

NAME _____ DATE _____

"Mask"erade

Make a mask out of a paper bag. On one side, show how you feel when you are scared. On the other side, show how you feel when you want to scare someone. Be prepared to explain your mask to someone else.

You may use any type of material you want to decorate or add to your mask if you want.

SKILL: *Interpreting Feelings*

NAME _____ DATE _____

A Poor Excuse Is Better Than None

Think of five acceptable excuses for not having your homework. Try to make them as creative and as original as you can!

Example: I could not do my homework because there was a big fire and my book burned.

I could not do my homework because:

1. _____

2. _____

3. _____

4. _____

5. _____

SKILL: *Cause/Effect*

NAME _____ DATE _____

Abbreviated Animal

Design your own abbreviated animal by making one part of the animal shorter than it should be.

Example: a dog with a tail that has been shortened — or abbreviated

Now look in a newspaper or magazine and find as many abbreviations as you can. Paste those abbreviations inside your abbreviated animal.

Choose five of your abbreviations and write the words for them on the back of your animal. Can you find someone who knows what part of the animal has been abbreviated **and** what the five abbreviations stand for?

SKILL: *Abbreviations*

NAME _____ DATE _____

Yourtown, U.S.A.

What's in a Name?

Write the name of your city and state. See how many abbreviations you can find beginning with the letters in your city and state. You may invite your whole family to help you with this one!

SKILL: *Abbreviations*

NAME _____ DATE _____

Geographical Genius

Look on an old map. Find and copy five
abbreviations. Now write the word for which
the abbreviation stands.

Abbreviation   *Word*

_____   _____

_____   _____

_____   _____

_____   _____

_____   _____

SKILL: *Abbreviations*

NAME _____ DATE _____

Cut It Out!

Look in a newspaper and find the following
abbreviations. Cut and paste them on the
blank lines below.

a day of the week _____

a month of the year _____

the initials of a person _____

a street, a road, or an avenue _____

a country, city, or state _____

a title of a person _____

SKILL: *Abbreviations*

NAME _____   DATE _____

Dream House

Search the classified ads for the house of your dream. Glue the ad in the space below. Circle each of the abbreviations and try to guess what each one means.

NAME _____   DATE _____

In Brief

Write your first, middle, and last initials. See how many abbreviations you can find beginning with your initials. Note that not all abbreviations begin with capital letters.

Example: S   Sept.   D Dr.
            A   Ave.   O oz.
            M Mon.   Y yd.

NAME _____ DATE _____

Street Wise

Streets can be called by many different
terms. Think of synonyms for the word *street*,
and write them below. Then go back and see
if you can write the abbreviation for each
synonym.

Example: Road – Rd.

SKILL: *Abbreviations*

NAME _____ DATE _____

News Briefs

Clip an article from a newspaper or
magazine. Circle all the abbreviations. Now
write the abbreviations and the words for
which they stand. You may glue your article
on this page if you have room.

SKILL: *Abbreviations*

NAME _____ DATE _____

Picturesque

Look in a magazine and find a picture you like. Either paste it here
or onto another piece of paper. Now write down all of the nouns you
can find in your picture. Remember, nouns are naming words and
name persons, places, or things.

SKILL: *Common Nouns*

NAME _____ DATE _____

Newsworthy Nouns

Listen to the national news tonight. See if
you can hear the names of national leaders.
Write down the names of those leaders and
their countries. Remember, names of people
and places are proper nouns and must

always begin with a _____ letter.

SKILL: *Proper Nouns*

NAME _____ DATE _____

Traction Action

Put on your sneakers and see how many
things you can *do* with them on. List some
things below.

Example: run

_____   _____

_____   _____

_____   _____

_____

BONUS: Now take your sneakers off. What
can you do barefoot that you can't do with
sneakers on? Write some of those verbs on
the back side of this sheet or on another
sheet of paper.

SKILL: *Verbs*

NAME _____ DATE _____

What's in a Name?

Make an acrostic with your name. Try to use
only adjectives.

Calvin Smith's Example:

C	*c* lever	S	*s* mart
A	*a* nxious	M	*m* annerly
L	*l* ovable	I	*i* nteresting
V	*v* ivacious	T	*t* all
I	*i* ntelligent	H	*h* ealthy
N	*n* eat		

Now it's your turn.

SKILL: *Adjectives*

NAME _____ DATE _____

Adverb Advantage

Cut out a picture and paste it on another sheet of paper. Now write a
verb that would fit an action in the picture. Next write down all the
words you can think of that tell *how* or *when*. These words are
adverbs. Underline all the *how* words and circle all the *when* words.

Example: In a picture of dancers, the verb could be *dance*. Words for
how could be *carefully* and *quickly*. Words for *when* could be *early*
and *yesterday*.

SKILL: Adverbs

NAME _____ DATE _____

Unsightly Search

You suddenly realize that you are invisible. Give directions to a
family member telling him/her where to find you. Underline a
prepositional phrase in each of your clues. You may use only five
clues.

Example: Come *in the front door.*   Go *to the hallway.*

_____

_____

_____

_____

_____

_____

SKILL: Prepositions

NAME _____ DATE _____

Leaf Relief

Glue a leaf in the space below. Now write
five adjectives to describe your leaf. Watch
your spelling.

SKILL: *Adjectives*

NAME _____ DATE _____

Proper Place

Look in the newspaper for proper nouns.
Write your proper nouns under the correct
headings.

Person	*Place*	*Thing*
_____	_____	_____
_____	_____	_____
_____	_____	_____
_____	_____	_____
_____	_____	_____
_____	_____	_____

SKILL: *Proper Nouns*

NAME _____ DATE _____

First Impressions

Find five adjectives and write them to look
like their meanings.

SKILL: *Adjectives*

NAME _____ DATE _____

Clowning Around

Describe your favorite clown at the circus.
Just fill in the necessary adjectives. (You may
use more than one adjective.)

    My clown has

_____ face

_____ eyes

_____ nose

_____ mouth

_____ body

_____ hair

_____ hat

_____ feet

Draw a picture of your clown.

SKILL: *Adjectives*

NAME _____ DATE _____

Probing for Pronouns

Read a sports article in the newspaper. Find
five pronouns and draw a line from the
pronoun to the person to whom it refers.

NAME _____ DATE _____

Homework Hunt

Look in the newspaper for each one of these
items. Be sure to write each down on the
blank.

a proper noun

_____

a common noun

_____

a pronoun

_____

a verb

_____

an adjective

_____

an adverb

_____

a preposition

_____

NAME _____   DATE _____

Rainbow Words

Cut out an action picture from a magazine. With your red crayon
write a verb that goes with that picture. With your blue crayon write
all the words that tell how. With your green crayon write all the
words that tell when. How many adverbs did you find? _____
Hint: Words that tell how and when are adverbs.
Be sure to clip the picture to this paper.

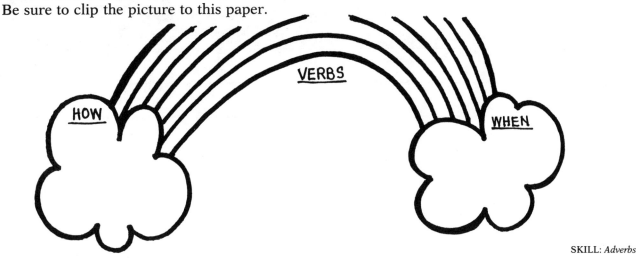

SKILL: *Adverbs*

NAME _____   DATE _____

Noun Knowledge

Look in your newspaper or magazine and
find things that do the following. Write the
name of each thing on the right blank.

talks _____

runs _____

flies _____

turns _____

shines _____

sings _____

squeaks _____

SKILL: *Nouns*

NAME _____ DATE _____

Vera Vegetable

Cut out a magazine picture of foods to create a Vera Vegetable
character. Glue them to another piece of paper and add features.
Below write five questions you would like to ask Vera. Don't forget
how asking sentences begin and end!

_____

_____

_____

_____

_____

SKILL: *Asking Sentences*

NAME _____ DATE _____

Super Shopper

Look in a catalog and find four things you would get for each
member of your family. Write those items below in *complete
sentences*. Be sure to make a careful selection and get things that
your family members really want.

Hint: Don't forget commas when putting items in a series.

_____

_____

_____

_____

SKILL: *Punctuation*

NAME _____ DATE _____

Jet Setting

You have won a free ticket on Continent Airlines. You can go to any country or city that begins with the letter ____. List below the places you would go. Underline those not in the USA.

_____

_____

_____

_____

_____

_____

_____

SKILL: *Capitalization*

NAME _____ DATE _____

What's in a Book?

Look in some of your favorite books. Find some words that begin with capital letters. Write down these words. Why are they capitalized?

_____

_____

_____

_____

_____

SKILL: *Capitalization*

NAME _____ DATE _____

Sentence Search

Look in a book. Locate and copy an example of each of the following types of sentences.

a declaratory sentence

_____

an exclamatory sentence

_____

an interrogative sentence

_____

a complex sentence

_____

a compound sentence

_____

_____

SKILL: *Sentence Review*

NAME _____ DATE _____

Scavenger Hunt

Look at a map or atlas and find examples of the following:

a river _____

a mountain range _____

an ocean _____

a city _____

a park/forest _____

a lake _____

a state _____

a capital _____

SKILL: *Capital Letters*

NAME _____ DATE _____

Tally Ho!

Cut out one small story from a magazine or
newspaper. Circle all the punctuation marks
you can find. How many of each did you
circle?

periods _____

question marks _____

apostrophes _____

quotation marks _____

exclamation points _____

commas _____

Attach your story to this sheet.

SKILL: *Punctuation Review*

NAME _____ DATE _____

Asking the Right Questions

Cut out a picture of someone you would love
to know more about. Attach the picture to
this sheet. Write five questions you would ask
that person.

_____

_____

_____

_____

_____

SKILL: *Question Marks*

NAME _____ DATE _____

Questionable Homework

Choose *one* of the words below and write as
many questions about the word as you can
think of. Try to begin your questions with as
many different words as possible.

    cow   refrigerator   clock   television   jam

_____

_____

_____

_____

_____

_____

SKILL: Question Marks

NAME _____ DATE _____

Help Wanted

Look in the classified ads and find a job that interests you. Write
three questions you would want to ask the employer. Write three
questions you think the employer will ask you.

Your Questions:

_____

_____

_____

Employer's Questions:

_____

_____

_____

SKILL: Question Marks

NAME _____ DATE _____

You Tell the Story!

Look at a cartoon. Now give it a title that would let the reader know what the main idea would be.

_____

(title)

BONUS Write a story about the cartoon on another sheet of paper.

SKILL: *Main Idea*

NAME _____ DATE _____

What's It All About?

Cut out a paragraph from a newspaper or magazine story. Glue that paragraph onto this sheet. Now write a headline that tells the main idea of your paragraph. Remember, when you write a headline, you may leave out small, unimportant words.

SKILL: *Main Idea*

NAME _____   DATE _____

Wheel of Sports

In the middle of a separate piece of paper, draw a circle. Add a smaller circle in the center and write the name of your favorite sport or hobby. Now draw lines coming out of the circle, and write one detail about the topic on each line.

Example:

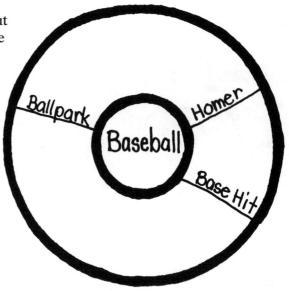

SKILL: *Details*

_____

NAME _____   DATE _____

Finding the Nitty Gritty

Cut out a headline from the newspaper or a magazine and paste it below. Now list five details that would support this headline.

SKILL: *Details*

NAME _____   DATE _____

Cereal Tidbits

A topic sentence summarizes the details in the rest of the paragraph. Read the following topic sentence. Then look in your cupboard and write a sentence giving a detail about each cereal you find. (If you can't find any cereals, you may pretend your favorite ones are there.)

Topic Sentence: There are many different kinds of breakfast cereals.

_____

_____

_____

_____

SKILL: *Details*

NAME _____   DATE _____

It's Classified!

Find the For Sale section of the classified ads in your newspaper. Locate something for sale that you would really like to have. Glue that ad here and answer these questions.

What is for sale?

_____

Who is selling it?

_____

How much does it cost?

_____

Where can you go to see it?

_____

What is the phone number?

_____

Find and circle two adjectives (describing words) in the ad.

SKILL: *Details*

NAME _____ DATE _____ _____

Shapes of Things to Come

Using only triangles, circles, and rectangles, invent a machine and
draw it on another sheet of paper. On the lines below, write a
paragraph telling what the machine does and who would buy it.

SKILL: *Paragraphs*

NAME _____ DATE _____

Scientifically Sound

Pretend you are a scientist. What would you
invent, and what would it do?

_____

_____

_____

_____

_____

_____

_____

SKILL: *Paragraphs*

NAME _____ DATE _____

Paragraph Particulars

Cut out from the newspaper a short
paragraph, a long paragraph, a paragraph
containing dialogue (people talking), and a
paragraph containing descriptions. Attach
those paragraphs to this sheet. Now
underline the main idea in each paragraph.

SKILL: Paragraphs

NAME _____ DATE _____

Jake the Flake

Jake the Flake is a rather strange individual. Only you know just how
very strange he really is. Tell about him in three paragraphs. In
paragraph one, tell what Jake did yesterday. In paragraph two, tell
what Jake is doing right now. In paragraph three, tell what Jake will
do tomorrow.

_____

_____

_____

_____

_____

_____

_____

SKILL: Paragraphs

NAME _____ DATE _____

Puppy Love

Read the "Pets for Sale" section in the
classified ads. Now write an ad to find a
home for this puppy.

_____

_____

_____

_____

BONUS: On another sheet of paper, write
what this puppy might be saying to make
someone want to take the puppy to the
person's home.

SKILL: *Miscellaneous Creations*

NAME _____ DATE _____

Every Litter Bit Helps!

Design a bumper sticker to discourage
littering. Make it as colorful and as catchy as
you can!

SKILL: *Miscellaneous Creations*

NAME _____ DATE _____

Quotable Quotes

Write what you think each person is saying.

The lost little child cried, "_____

_____."

"_____?"

asked the teacher.

My dad yelled, "_____

_____!"

The Man in the Moon said, "_____

_____."

SKILL: *Quotations*

NAME _____ DATE _____

Happy Birthday!

It's time to have your birthday party. Design an invitation you can send. Be sure to tell your guests what kind of party it is, when, and where the party will be, and whom the party is for.

_____

_____

_____

_____

_____

_____

SKILL: *Invitations*

NAME _____ DATE _____

Character Collage

Select a person you see often, such as your mother, father, sister, brother, teacher, or friend. Cut out pictures from newspapers, magazines, or catalogs that help describe the character you chose. The pictures might show what that person does, how he or she looks, or how he or she acts. On another piece of paper paste the pictures in a collage. Be sure to give a title to your creation.

SKILL: *Miscellaneous Creation*

NAME _____ DATE _____

Letter Perfect

Write a letter to a make-believe friend who lives in Alaska. Put many mistakes in the letter and ask your mom or your dad or another older person to check it for you. Give that person a hug for every mistake he or she can find.

_____
Heading

_____
Greeting

_____

_____

_____

_____

_____
Closing

How many hugs did they get?____   _____
Signature

SKILL: *Letter Writing*

NAME _____ DATE _____

Happy Holiday

Create a new holiday. Tell when it will be celebrated, how it will be celebrated, and who will be honored. Design a banner or poster publicizing your new holiday.

SKILL: *Creative Thinking*

NAME _____ DATE _____

Up Close and Personal

Make a collage in the space below. Use only words that tell about you. Make sure you can read all the words.

SKILL: *Self-description*

NAME _____ DATE _____

T-Time Design

Listen to the news. Pick an individual and design a T-shirt which
expresses that individual's point of view.

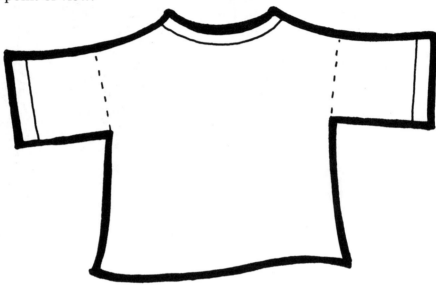

SKILL: *Character Traits*

NAME _____ DATE _____

Tombstone Territory

Design an epitaph to go on a tombstone. Try
to make the epitaph rhyme.

Example: Here lies Grover.
            He was run over.

SKILL: *Rhyming*

NAME _____ DATE _____

Cartoon Capers

Watch a cartoon on television. Now list three
things you saw in that cartoon that could not
really happen.

1. _____

_____

2. _____

_____

3. _____

_____

BONUS Draw pictures of one or more of your
sentences on another sheet of paper.

SKILL: *Realism/Fantasy*

NAME _____ DATE _____

"Inch"ing to Be Taller

You are only one inch tall. *Where* could you
go? *What* can you do? Would it be fun to be
that tall, or would it be rather dangerous?

Write a paragraph about being an inch tall.
(Don't forget the title for your paragraph!)

_____

_____

_____

_____

SKILL: *Realism/Fantasy*

NAME _____ DATE _____

An Unbelievable Story

Cut out an interesting headline. Make up a
story to go with that headline that could not
happen in real life. Remember what makes a
story make-believe.

_____

_____

_____

_____

_____

_____

_____

SKILL: *Realism/Fantasy*

NAME _____ DATE _____

Super Powers

Write down some **real** things about yourself. Now write down three
or more powers you would like to have if you suddenly became a
make-believe character. Don't forget to use complete sentences!

_____

_____

_____

_____

_____

_____

Guten Morgen, Freundin!

LINGOKID

Bonjour monamis!

Buenos días, amigos!

SKILL: *Realism/Fantasy*

NAME _____ DATE _____

A Perfect Pair

Select one boy and one girl in your classroom. First write one
paragraph about the boy, telling what you like about him. Then write
a paragraph telling what you like about the girl.

_____

_____

_____

_____

_____

_____

_____

_____

SKILL: *Critical Thinking*

NAME _____ DATE _____

Your Opinion, Please

Give your opinion about one of these subjects. Be sure to tell why you
think as you do. Write your editorial on another sheet of paper.

1. Elementary students should or should not be able to vote for the
    president of the USA.
2. Elementary students should or should not have homework.
3. Seventeen-year-olds should or should not drive school buses.
4. Our school needs a new _____. Why?

SKILL: *Critical Thinking*

NAME _____ DATE _____

A Year Without Sunshine

Cut out a picture in which you know the sun is shining. Now tell five or more things that might happen if the sun did not shine for one year.

SKILL: *Critical Thinking*

NAME _____ DATE _____

Friend or Foe

Look in the newspaper or a magazine and cut out a picture of a famous person. Would you like to have this person as a friend? Explain why or why not.

_____

_____

_____

_____

_____

_____

_____

_____

SKILL: *Critical Thinking*

NAME _____ DATE _____

Trash to Treasures

Look in your kitchen trash can. List items which could be recycled.

_____   _____

_____   _____

_____   _____

_____   _____

_____   _____

How does recycling help the environment?

_____

_____

SKILL: *Critical Thinking*

NAME _____ DATE _____

Sink or Swim

The faucet in your bathtub won't shut off, and water is rapidly filling the tub. It is 9 o'clock on Saturday night. Look in the yellow pages and select three plumbers you could call for help. Write down their names and phone numbers. Be sure to select the ones that are closest to your home.

_____

_____

_____

_____

_____

_____

SKILL: *Critical Thinking*

NAME _____ DATE _____

Table Topics

Look at a table of contents in a magazine. Write down five or more facts you can find out by using this table.

_____

_____

_____

_____

_____

Now write down one thing the table of contents does not tell you.

_____

_____

SKILL: *Reference Sources/Table of Contents*

NAME _____ DATE _____

Mapping It Out

Japan is an island. Using a map or an atlas, name five other islands. Write where you can find each of these islands.

Example: Japan is near Korea in the Pacific Ocean.

1. _____   3. _____

   _____   _____

2. _____   4. _____

   _____   _____

                                    5. _____

                                       _____

SKILL: *Reference Sources/Maps*

NAME _____ DATE _____

Look It Up!

What does the word *protest* mean? Look in your dictionary to learn its meaning. List some causes you would protest.

Example: I would protest school on Saturday.

_____

_____

_____

BONUS What are the guide words on that page?

_____

Would you find the word *party* on that page? Why or why not?

_____

SKILL: *Reference Sources/Dictionary*

NAME _____ DATE _____

Favorite Food Facts

Look in the grocery ads in the newspaper
and find a fruit or vegetable that you really
like to eat. Now look in the encyclopedia and
write five facts about this food that you did
not know before.

_____

_____

_____

_____

_____

_____

_____

SKILL: *Reference Sources/Encyclopedia*

NAME _____ DATE _____

Calling Codes

Look in the front of your telephone directory. Find the map of the United States that shows the area codes. Find the area codes for these places.

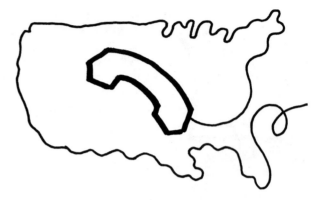

1. Dallas, Texas _____

2. State of Maine _____

3. Jacksonville, Florida _____

4. Atlanta, Georgia _____

5. State of Idaho _____

6. Chicago, Illinois _____

7. Albany, New York _____

8. State of Nevada _____

9. State of Rhode Island _____

10. State of Alabama _____

SKILL: *Reference Sources/Telephone Directory*

NAME _____ DATE _____

Dream Machine

Look in the classified section of the newspaper and find your dream car. Write down the following information about it. Include a drawing or a picture of this car.

Make _____

Year _____

Color _____

Price _____

Address of seller _____
          or
Phone number _____

How could you earn money to buy this car?

SKILL: *Reference Sources/Classified Ads*

NAME _____ DATE _____

Strawberry Search

Look in the index in one of your mon's cook books and see how many recipes you can find that use strawberries as an ingredient. Write down some of those recipes and the page on which you would find them. Underline the recipe you would most like to prepare.

_____

_____

_____

_____

_____

_____

SKILL: *Reference Sources/Index*

NAME _____ DATE _____

Calendar Check

Find a calendar for the present year and answer the following:

1. On what day of the week will your birthday come this year? Next year?

_____

2. You are baby-sitting every Saturday and Sunday during the month of July. How many days will you be working? What are those dates?

_____

3. Christmas vacation will begin this year on December 19. What day will this be?

_____

4. Months were named for different things. Look up January in your encyclopedia, and tell in a short paragraph on another sheet of paper how January got its name.

SKILL: *Reference Source/Calendar*

NAME _____ DATE _____

Let Your Fingers Do the Walking

Use the yellow pages to find out how many
public schools are in your city. Find out how
many of them are the following:

elementary schools _____

middle schools or
junior high schools _____

high schools _____

Now make a bar graph using the
information you found.

SKILL: *Reference Sources/Telephone Directory*

NAME _____ DATE _____

Take a Trip

Plan a vacation to a place you would like to
visit. Look at a map and locate the names of
five places you would go through to get to
your vacation site. List these locations in
alphabetical order.

MT. LEBLEU
5,962 FT.

SKILL: *Reference Sources/Maps*

NAME _____ DATE _____

Did You Know?

Our country has many great leaders. Select your favorite. Find five or more facts about him or her that your parents don't know. Use your encyclopedia to help you.

_____

_____

_____

_____

_____

_____

_____

_____

_____

SKILL: *Encyclopedia*

NAME _____ DATE _____

What's Inside?

Look at a table of contents in a magazine. Write down five or more topics that are covered in this issue.

BONUS Write down one topic that is not covered.

_____   _____

_____   _____

_____   _____

_____   _____

_____   _____

Now alphabetize those topics. Put a 1 by the one that will come first, a 2 by the second one, and continue until all your topics are numbered. Use a separate sheet of paper if you need to.

SKILL: *Reference Sources/Table of Contents*

NAME _____ DATE _____

What's My Line?

Find a career for each clue.

1. A job that has a short vowel

_____

2. A job that has a long vowel

_____

3. A job that is a compound word

_____

4. A job that has three syllables

_____

5. A job that begins with a blend

_____

6. A job that has a prefix

_____

7. A job that has a suffix

_____

8. A job you would like to have in twenty

years _____

HOLIDAYS: *Labor Day*

NAME _____ DATE _____

Land Ahoy!

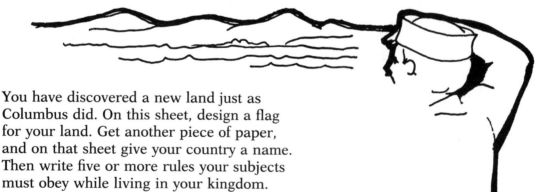

You have discovered a new land just as
Columbus did. On this sheet, design a flag
for your land. Get another piece of paper,
and on that sheet give your country a name.
Then write five or more rules your subjects
must obey while living in your kingdom.

HOLIDAYS: *Columbus Day*

NAME _____ DATE _____

Hair-Raising Words

This is nothing to be frightened about! Locate these Halloween words in your dictionary. Write down the guide words that are on the same page where you found these words.

Guide Words

1. ghost   _____   _____
2. witch   _____   _____
3. eerie   _____   _____
4. goblin   _____   _____
5. costume   _____   _____

BONUS Is *eerie* something you wear? _____

HOLIDAYS: *Halloween*

NAME _____ DATE _____

Boo-ish on Words

List as many Halloween words as you can think of, and write them in the ghost below.

Underline the **"spooooky"** words in orange.

HOLIDAYS: *Halloween*

NAME _____   DATE _____

Safety First

Halloween is a time of the year when you
must remember safety rules. Write down
some safety rules that you think your
classmates should follow.

_____

_____

_____

_____

_____

Now go back and number them in the order
of their importance to you. Put the number 1
by the rule you feel is most important, 2 by
the next one, and so on. Do you follow all of
these rules?

HOLIDAYS: *Halloween*

NAME _____   DATE _____

A Bracing Brew

You are in charge of the witches' brew this
Halloween. You can include only ingredients
having _____ syllables. List your ingredients
below. Now tell the proper sequence for
making your delightful Halloween creation.

_____

_____

_____

_____

_____

If you need more room, use another sheet of
paper.

HOLIDAYS: *Halloween*

NAME _____ DATE _____

What's for Dinner?

You need to help shop for the Thanksgiving feast. What items will you need from these departments in the grocery store?

Dairy	*Produce*	*Bread*	*Canned Goods*
_____	_____	_____	_____
_____	_____	_____	_____
_____	_____	_____	_____
_____	_____	_____	_____

How much do you think the

grocery bill will be? _____

HOLIDAYS: *Thanksgiving*

NAME _____ DATE _____

Thankful Thoughts

Trace your hand on another sheet of paper. Complete the sentence "I am thankful for . . ." on each of the fingers. Don't forget your thumb, too!

Example: I am thankful for my parents.

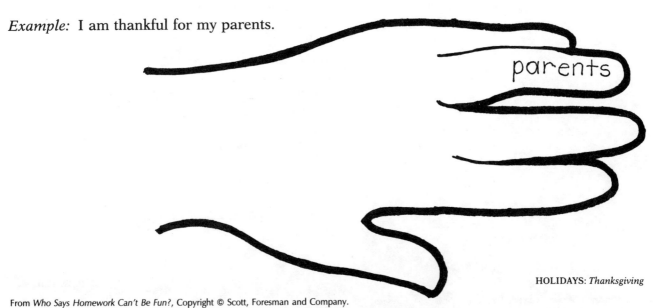

HOLIDAYS: *Thanksgiving*

NAME _____   DATE _____

Suited for Santa

You have been selected to create a new suit for Santa. Describe how that new suit will look and why you have designed it the way you did.

_____

_____

_____

_____

_____

_____

If you need more space, use another sheet of paper.

HOLIDAYS: *Christmas*

NAME _____   DATE _____

Ho! Ho! Ho!

Can you figure out these words?
They all have a *ho* in them.

a Christmas plant with red berries: h o__ __ __
a kind of ice cream and cake: __ h o __ __ __ __ __ __
not tall: __ h o __ __
a sticker on a rose: __ h o __ __
a tramp: h o __ __
truthful: h o __ __ __ __
word for a store: __ h o __
all the parts of the pizza: __ h o __ __
where you go after school: h o __ __
place to learn: __ __ h o __ __
MERRY CHRISTMAS!!

How many *ho! ho! ho!* words did you get? _____

HOLIDAYS: *Christmas*

NAME _____   DATE _____

Trimming the Tree

Here you see a tree that needs to be decorated.
You can decorate it by adding a noun on
each branch and an adjective in each ball.
Can you "trim the tree"?

BONUS Can you use all three-syllable
Christmas words?

HOLIDAYS: *Christmas*

NAME _____   DATE _____

You Light Up My Life

Look at the letters on the Menorah. Can you think of a gift you would
like to have that begins with the letter on each candle? Light up the
Menorah by writing the name of a gift on each line.

BONUS On another sheet of paper, make all
the singular words plural.

HOLIDAYS: *Hanukkah*

NAME _____ DATE _____

Happy New Year . . . for Whom?

You have been asked by your teacher to make her New Year's
Resolutions for her. Using complete sentences, write down these
resolutions the way you would like them to read.

_____

_____

_____

_____

_____

If your teacher followed these resolutions, how would the remaining
part of the year be for you? Use another sheet of paper to write your
answer.

HOLIDAYS: *New Year's Day*

NAME _____ DATE _____

The 100th Day

Today is the **100th** day of school. How many things can you do at
school that begin with the following letters?

a _____   b _____   c _____

d _____   e _____   f _____

g _____   h _____   i _____

j _____   k _____   l _____

m _____   n _____   o _____

p _____   q _____   r _____

s _____   t _____   u _____

v _____   w/x _____   y/z _____

All of these words are *doing* words. Do you know what they are called? _____   HOLIDAYS: *The 100th Day*

NAME _____ DATE _____

Content of Character

Dr. Martin Luther King, Jr., was a true leader in peace and a friend to many. Create a special award to be presented to the friendliest or nicest person in your classroom. Be sure to put your classmate's name on the award, and tell why he or she deserves the award.

My Award:

HOLIDAYS: *Martin Luther King's Birthday*

NAME _____ DATE _____

Presidential Promise

Abraham Lincoln was known as "Honest Abe" because he was so truthful. If you were to become president of your class, what are some promises you would make to the students? Try to make promises you could keep! (Watch your spelling!)

_____

_____

_____

_____

_____

_____

_____

HOLIDAYS: *President's Day*

NAME _____ DATE _____

You're Number One!

You've been elected the first child president of the United States.
Wow! What will be your first bill to ask congress to pass?

_____

_____

What country will you first visit, and what will you tell that country's
leaders?

_____

_____

Which of the presidents of the United States do you hope to be most
like? Why?

_____

_____

_____

HOLIDAYS: *Presidents' Day*

NAME _____ DATE _____

Presidential Homework

In your coins, find four quarters. Toss one quarter at a time into a
pot. Count how much money is in the pot. Circle your answer:

   $.25 $.50 $.75 $1.00

How many times did George Washington's face show up? _____

Which would you rather have, two quarters or three dimes? Why?

_____

What could you buy for four quarters?

_____

   Would George Washington have been able to buy the same thing as you can for four
quarters? Why, or why not?

_____

_____

_____

HOLIDAYS: *Presidents' Day*

NAME _____ DATE _____

Downright Hoggish

If the groundhog sees his shadow, spring is delayed. List some things you can do in the spring which you cannot do during colder weather.

_____

_____

_____

What are some signs that spring is on its way?

_____

_____

_____

HOLIDAYS: *Groundhog Day*

NAME _____ DATE _____

Picturesque for Pete

Open your newspaper to the editorial page, and find these letters somewhere on the page.

G R O U N D H O G   D A Y

Try to find some of them at the top, some in the middle, and some near the bottom of the page. Put a big dot on each letter as you find it.

Now go back and connect your dots. Look at the design you have made, and use it to make a picture of something Pete the Groundhog might see if the sun was shining when he came out of his hole on Groundhog Day.

HOLIDAYS: *Groundhog Day*

NAME _____ DATE _____

Love at First Bite!

You are inventing a new type of chocolate,
and you want to create an advertisement for
your chocolates that will make everyone
want to buy a box of them for his or her
Valentine. Write your ad here, and
remember to use lots of adjectives!

BONUS Draw a picture of your luscious
creation!

HOLIDAYS: *Valentine's Day*

NAME _____ DATE _____

Straight to the Heart

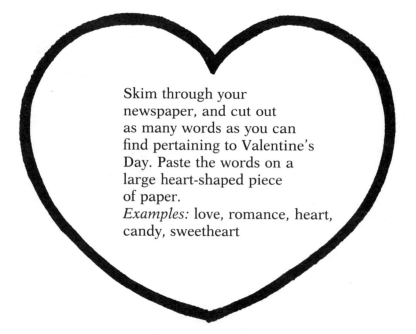

Skim through your
newspaper, and cut out
as many words as you can
find pertaining to Valentine's
Day. Paste the words on a
large heart-shaped piece
of paper.
Examples: love, romance, heart,
candy, sweetheart

HOLIDAYS: *Valentine's Day*

NAME _____   DATE _____

Hearty Homework

It's time to write your valentines. Attached is our class list. Put all the girls' names and boys' names in alphabetical order below.

Girls

_____

_____

_____

_____

_____

_____

Boys

_____

_____

_____

_____

_____

_____

HOLIDAYS: *Valentine's Day*

NAME _____   DATE _____

Irish Cook-Off

Create a recipe for one of these St. Patrick's Day foods:

Shamrock Salad   Irish Stew
Leprechaun Leftovers   Clover Cupcakes
St. Pat's Punch   Blarney Stone Soup

Be sure to tell us what the ingredients are in your recipe and how to prepare it. You may need these words: cup, tablespoon, mix, stir, pour, beat, bake, cook, degrees, minutes, and oven.

Write your recipe below or on another piece of paper.

_____

_____

_____

_____

HOLIDAYS: *St. Patrick's Day*

NAME _____   DATE _____

Seeing Green

By golly, it's St. Patrick's Day. There's green
everywhere. Name five things that are always
green. Write a sentence using each word.
Good luck!

_____

_____

_____

_____

_____

_____

HOLIDAYS: *St. Patrick's Day*

NAME _____   DATE _____

Symbolic

The shamrock is a small three-leaf clover.
It's the national flower of Ireland. Look in an
encyclopedia or a history book and find your
state's flower. Write it here:

_____

Did you find any other state symbols? What
would you suggest for a state insect? Why?
What does the insect look like?

_____

_____

_____

_____

HOLIDAYS: *St. Patrick's Day*

NAME _____ DATE _____

Spring Fling

Use an encyclopedia to find some interesting facts about spring.

_____

_____

_____

_____

_____

Now pretend you are an especially beautiful flower that can walk, talk, see, and hear. Use another sheet of paper to write a story about a day in your life.

HOLIDAYS: *First Day of Spring*

NAME _____ DATE _____

April Fool

Make up some foolish headlines to appear in the newspaper on April Fools' Day.

HOLIDAYS: *April Fools' Day*

NAME _____ DATE _____

"Egg"ceptional Eggs

You are to create a different type of Easter egg. Each of your eggs
will contain the name of a material that will float on water.
Experiment around your house and find objects that will float. Then
record them on the eggs.

BONUS Use your encyclopedia to find out why some objects float and
others sink. Be prepared to share your findings with the class.

HOLIDAYS: *Easter*

NAME _____ DATE _____

Scrambled Eggs

Many words will remind you of Easter. Write down as many as you
can think of and put them on another sheet of paper. Then scramble
the letters and write those letters inside the eggs. Can you find
anyone who can unscramble your eggs and figure out your Easter
words?

HOLIDAYS: *Easter*

NAME _____ DATE _____

Hats Off to You!

Because you did such a great job with your

homework, _____, you
may skip doing it tonight.

_____
Teacher

_____
Date

No Homework Permit

NAME _____ DATE _____

Happy Birthday to You!

Since this is your very special day,

_____, you may
select to skip your homework tonight.
Have a great day!

_____
Teacher

_____
Date

No Homework Permit

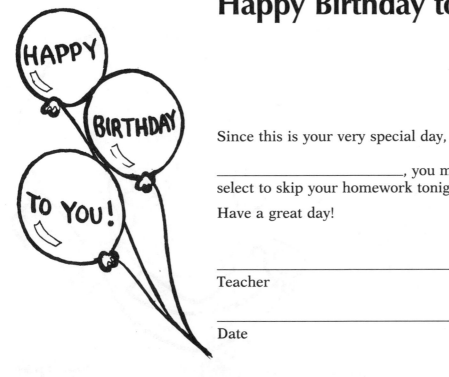

NAME _____ DATE _____

Keep on Shining!

I like your style, _____.
Because your work was so good, you
do not have to do any homework tonight.

_____
Teacher

_____
Date

No Homework Permit

NAME _____ DATE _____

Time Out!

You have done so well, _____.
You deserve a night off!

_____
Teacher

_____
Date

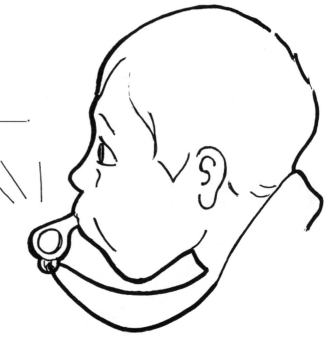

No Homework Permit

NAME _____ DATE _____

A Whale of a Job

You did a **whale** of a job on your homework today,

_____. You may take the night off!

_____
Teacher

_____
Date

No Homework Permit

NAME _____ DATE _____

This Little Bird

This little bird
Has come to say
That because your homework
Is so good today
You may have time off
And go out and play!

_____
Teacher

_____
Date

No Homework Permit

NAME ______________________________ DATE ______________

High Flier

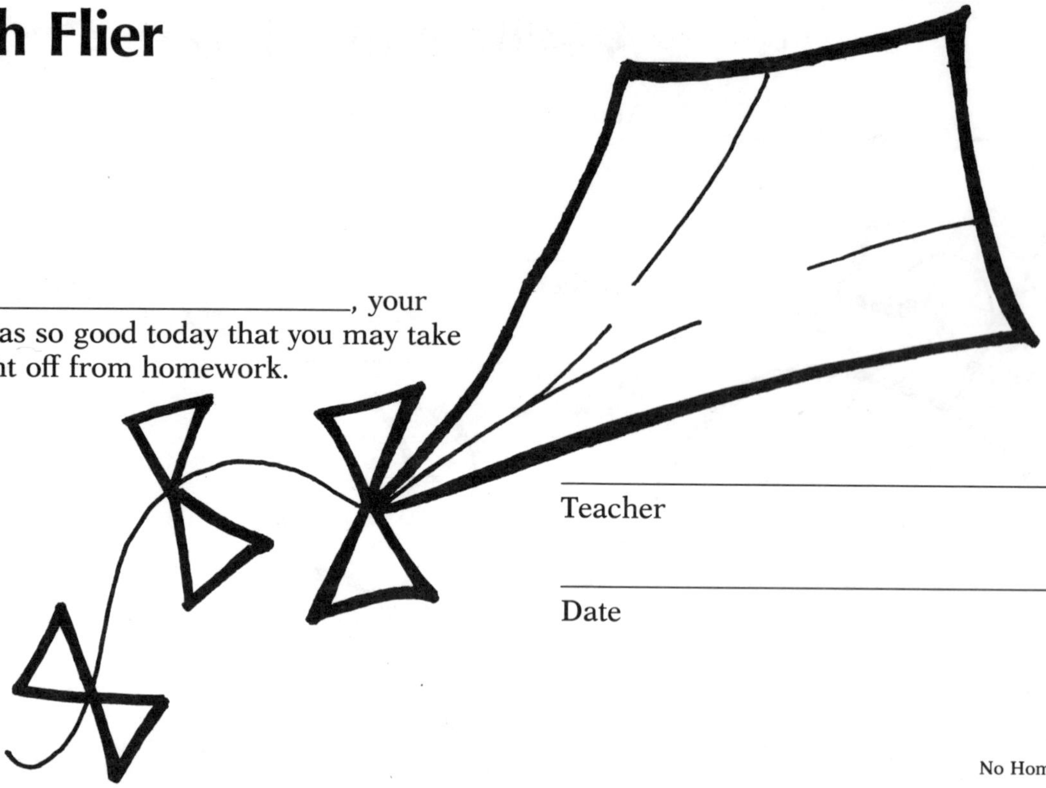

Wow, ______________________, your work was so good today that you may take the night off from homework.

____
Teacher

____
Date

No Homework Permit

NAME ______________________________ DATE ______________

Standing Tall

You're head and shoulders above the rest,

______________________. Because you have done such a good job, you have a night without homework.

____
Teacher

____
Date

No Homework Permit

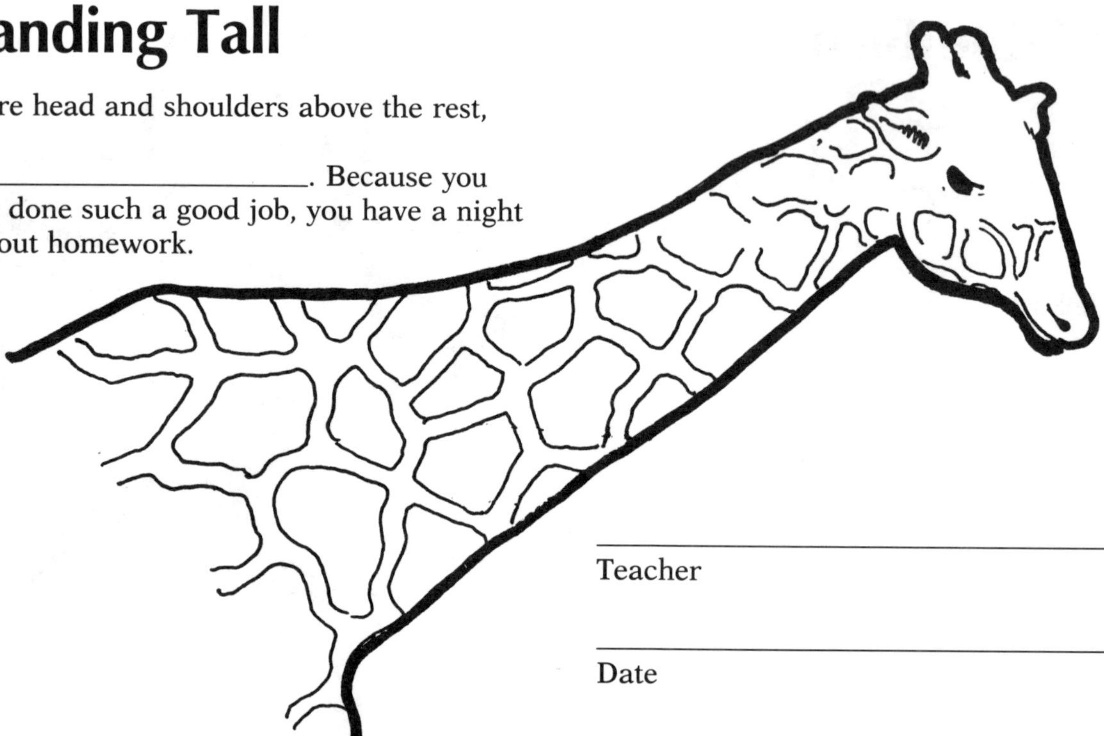

NAME _____ DATE _____

Take a Break

Roses are red
Violets are blue
Your homework was super
So you've nothing else to do!

Because of your excellent homework last night,

_____, you may take tonight off. Keep up the good work!

_____
Teacher

_____
Date

No Homework Permit

NAME _____ DATE _____

Moving On

Keep on trucking,

_____. Your homework was so good that you may skip it tonight.

_____
Teacher

_____
Date

No Homework Permit